This book is for

....

whose only handicap

is himself

A ROUND WITH...
A CORGI BOOK 0 552 99225 9

First publication in Great Britain

PRINTING HISTORY
Corgi edition published 1986
Copyright © Ian Heath 1986

Corgi Books are published by Transworld Publishers Ltd.,
61–63 Uxbridge Road, Ealing, London W5 5SA, in Australia by
Transworld Publishers (Australia) Pty. Ltd., 15–23 Helles
Avenue, Moorebank, NSW 2170, and in New Zealand by Transworld
Publishers (N.Z.) Ltd., Cnr. Moselle and Waipareira Avenues,
Henderson, Auckland.

Made and printed in West Germany by Mohndruck
Graphische Betriebe GmbH, Gütersloh

Ianheath's
A ROUND WITH

YORE GOLF CLUB

PLAYER............................... HANDICAP.......... DATE.............

HOLE	YARDS	PAR	STROKE INDEX	PLAYERS SCORE	WON LOST HALVED	HOLE	YARDS	PAR	STROKE INDEX	PLAYERS SCORE	WON LOST HALVED
1	361	4	12			10	425	4	4		
2	324	4	6			11	332	4	11		
3	392	4	10			12	149	3	15		
4	294	4	14			13	401	4	13		
5	452	4	2			14	395	4	8		
6	145	3	16			15	487	5	5		
7	422	4	3			16	151	3	17		
8	480	5	1			17	390	4	9		
9	136	3	18			18	402	4	7		
OUT	3006	35				IN	3132	35			
						OUT	3006	35			
						TOTAL	6138	70			
						HANDICAP					
						NET SCORE					

MARKERS SIGNATURE.................

PLAYERS SIGNATURE ....

1ˢᵀ   361 yards   PAR 4   1ˢᵀ STROKE

1ST   361 yards   PAR 4   2ND STROKE

1ST 361 yards PAR 4 3RD STROKE

1ˢᵗ   361 yards   Par 4   4ᵀᴴ STROKE

2ND   324 yards   PAR 4   1ST STROKE

2ND   324 yards   PAR 4   7TH STROKE

3RD 392 yards   PAR 4   8TH STROKE

3RD   392 yards   PAR 4   9TH STROKE

4TH   294 yards   PAR 4   2ND STROKE

4TH   294 yards   PAR 4   5TH STROKE

4TH   294 yards   PAR 4   6TH STROKE

5TH   452 yards   PAR 4   8TH STROKE ...

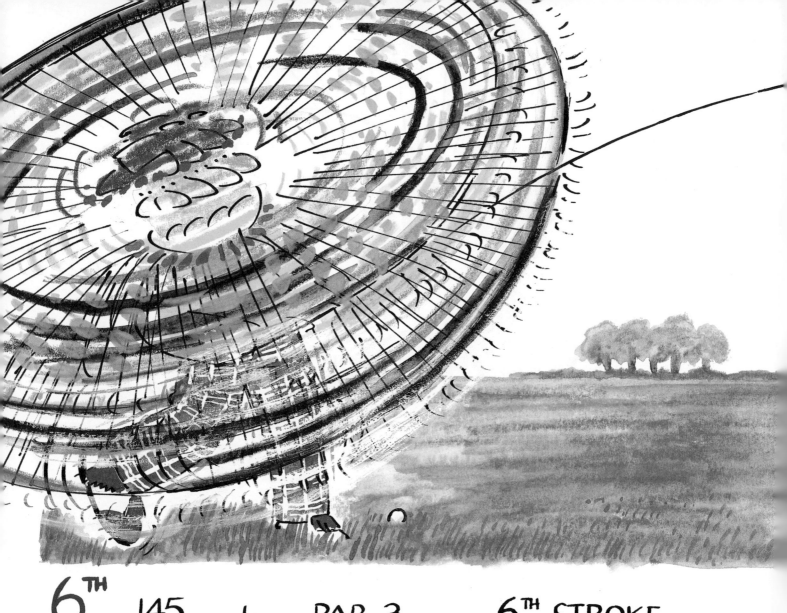

6TH   145 yards   PAR 3   6TH STROKE

7TH   422 yards   PAR 4   7TH STROKE

8TH   480 yards   PAR 5   6TH STROKE

9ᵀᴴ   136 yards   PAR 3   6ᵀᴴ STROKE

YORE GOLF CLUB

PLAYER............................... HANDICAP......... DATE.............

HOLE	YARDS	PAR	STROKE INDEX	PLAYERS SCORE	WON LOST HALVED	HOLE	YARDS	PAR	STROKE INDEX	PLAYERS SCORE	WON LOST HALVED
1	361	4	12	4	½	10	425	4	4		
2	324	4	6	9	L	11	332	4	11		
3	392	4	10	12	L	12	149	3	15		
4	294	4	14	9	L	13	401	4	13		
5	452	4	2	10	L	14	395	4	8		
6	145	3	16	7	L	15	487	5	5		
7	422	4	3	10	L	16	151	3	17		
8	480	5	1	8	L	17	390	4	9		
9	136	3	18	10	L	18	402	4	7		
OUT	3006	35		79		IN	3132	35			
						OUT	3006	35			
						TOTAL	6138	70			

MARKERS SIGNATURE ....

PLAYERS SIGNATURE ....

HANDICAP		
NET SCORE		

10TH   425 yards   PAR 4   7TH STROKE

11ᵀᴴ   332 yards   PAR 4   3ᴿᴰ STROKE.....

11TH   332 *yards*   PAR 4   6TH STROKE

12TH   149 yards   PAR 3   4TH STROKE

12TH   149 yards   PAR 3   6TH STROKE

12TH   149 yards   PAR 3   7TH STROKE

13TH   401 yards   PAR 4   6TH STROKE

13TH   401 yards   PAR 4   7TH STROKE

14TH   395 yards   PAR 4   3RD STROKE

14TH   395 yards   PAR 4

14TH   395 yards   PAR 4   8TH STROKE

15ᵀᴴ   487 yards   PAR 5   7ᵀᴴ STROKE

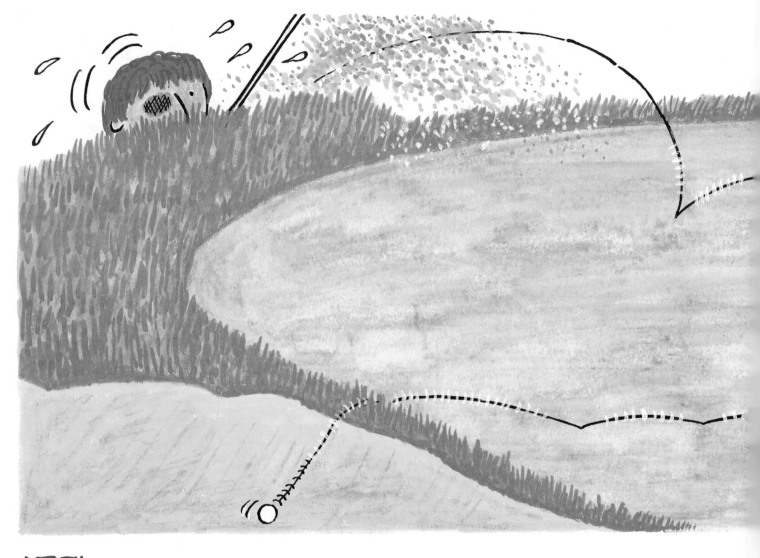

15ᵀᴴ   487 yards   PAR 5   10ᵀᴴ STROKE

16ᵀᴴ   151 yards   PAR 3   4ᵀᴴ STROKE

16TH 151 yards PAR 3 6TH STROKE

16TH 151 yards PAR 3 7TH STROKE

17TH 390 yards PAR 4   5TH STROKE

17TH   390 yards   PAR 4   7TH STROKE

18TH 402 yards PAR 4

18TH   402 yards   PAR 4   10TH STROKE

18ᵀᴴ   402 yards   PAR 4   11ᵀᴴ STROKE

YORE GOLF CLUB

PLAYER............................... HANDICAP.......... DATE.............

HOLE	YARDS	PAR	STROKE INDEX	PLAYERS SCORE	WON LOST HALVED	HOLE	YARDS	PAR	STROKE INDEX	PLAYERS SCORE	WON LOST HALVED
1	361	4	12	4	½	10	425	4	4	10	L
2	324	4	6	9	L	11	332	4	11	12	L
3	392	4	10	12	L	12	149	3	15	9	L
4	294	4	14	9	L	13	401	4	13	13	L
5	452	4	2	10	L	14	395	4	8	10	L
6	145	3	16	7	L	15	487	5	5	12	L
7	422	4	3	10	L	16	151	3	17	7	L
8	480	5	1	8	L	17	390	4	9	9	L
9	136	3	18	10	L	18	402	4	7	11	L
OUT	3006	35		79		IN	3132	35		93	
						OUT	3006	35		79	
						TOTAL	6138	70		172	

MARKERS SIGNATURE ....

PLAYERS SIGNATURE ....

HANDICAP		
NET SCORE